Cyber Security and AI

Mark Hayward

Published by Mark Hayward, 2025.

Table of Contents

Cyber Security & AI

About

    With over 23 years of cyber security expertise and a distinguished career in the UK Armed Forces, this author seamlessly blends military discipline with advanced industry knowledge. Having provided exceptional cyber security services to both local and central government departments, they are a recognized authority in safeguarding digital landscapes. Their unique approach makes complex concepts engaging and accessible, appealing to a diverse audience eager to understand the critical intersection of cyber security and artificial intelligence.

Table of Contents

1. Introduction to Cyber Security and AI

2. AI Technologies in Cyber Security

3. Benefits of AI in Cyber Security

4. Challenges of Implementing AI in Cyber Security

5. AI and Cyber Threat Landscape

6. Ethical Considerations in AI for Cyber Security

7. AI Tools for Cyber Security Professionals

8. Case Studies of AI in Cyber Security

1. Introduction to Cyber Security and AI

1.1 Understanding Cyber Security

Cyber security involves the practices, technologies, and processes designed to protect networks, devices, programs, and data from unauthorized access, damage, and attacks. As the digital landscape evolves, the importance of cyber security becomes increasingly critical. It safeguards sensitive information and maintains the integrity of systems against cyber threats such as hacking, malware, and data breaches. In today's interconnected world, where businesses and individuals rely heavily on technology, the implications of a security breach can be devastating, affecting finances, reputation, and trust. As artificial intelligence (AI) permeates our daily lives and business operations, it not only raises the stakes in the cyber security arena but also provides new tools for mitigating threats. Understanding how AI can enhance monitoring and response capabilities while also recognizing its potential vulnerabilities will shape the future of cyber security.

To grasp the full scope of cyber security, familiarity with key concepts and terminologies is essential. Terms like 'firewall,' 'malware,' 'phishing,' and 'encryption' form the backbone of the conversation about security measures and threats. Firewalls act as barriers to prevent unauthorized access, while malware refers to malicious software intended to harm or exploit any programmable device or network. Phishing techniques are deceptive tactics used to acquire sensitive information by masquerading as trustworthy entities. Encryption, on the other hand, transforms data into a secure format that cannot be easily read by unauthorized users, ensuring the confidentiality of information. As cyber threats grow more sophisticated, so too do the terminologies that describe them, reflecting an ever-evolving lexicon in the world of cyber security.

Diving deeper into the integration of artificial intelligence in cyber security, it is clear that AI algorithms can analyze vast amounts of data at incredible speeds, identifying patterns indicative of potential breaches more efficiently than human analysts. This predictive capability not only enhances threat detection but also aids in developing proactive security measures. However, as systems become increasingly automated, the risk of AI being exploited by cyber criminals also escalates. Malicious actors may use AI to launch more sophisticated attacks, creating a paradox where the same technology designed to protect can also be weaponized. Thus, professionals in the field must continually update their knowledge and skills to stay ahead of the evolving landscape. Emphasizing continuous learning and adaptation will be critical in harnessing AI's benefits while mitigating its risks.

1.2 The Rise of AI in Technology

The rapid advancement of AI technologies has significantly transformed various industries over the last decade. From healthcare to finance, AI tools are being developed and implemented at an unprecedented pace. In the healthcare sector, AI algorithms can analyze medical images faster and more accurately than human professionals, providing early diagnoses and reducing the burdens on medical staff. In finance, AI has revolutionized fraud detection, employing complex machine learning models to analyze transaction patterns and flag anomalies in real-time. Retailers use AI to enhance inventory management, personalize customer experiences, and streamline supply chain operations, demonstrating its versatility and importance across multiple fields. As these advancements continue to proliferate, the implications for the workplace, labour markets, and service delivery mechanisms are substantial, heralding an era where AI is an integral part of everyday business operations.

The growth of AI has also sparked numerous innovations that have reshaped technological workflows. For instance, the automation of repetitive tasks allows employees to focus on more strategic initiatives, increasing overall productivity. Businesses integrate AI-driven analytics tools to derive insights from massive data sets, leading to better decision-making processes. Moreover, AI is enhancing software development through smart coding assistants that suggest code snippets and identify bugs, significantly accelerating project timelines. These changes signify how AI is not merely an adjunct to existing technologies but a driving force that reimagines workflows, enhances efficiencies, and pushes the boundaries of what is possible. For professionals in cybersecurity, understanding these dynamics is critical, as the integration of AI in technology also brings a new set of challenges. The same systems that improve business operations can also create vulnerabilities, making it essential for cybersecurity experts to adapt their strategies to defend against AI-driven threats.

As AI continues to evolve and pervade various technologies, cybersecurity professionals must prepare for a landscape where both opportunities and threats are intrinsically linked to these advancements. To stay ahead, embracing AI tools for proactive threat detection and response rather than solely focusing on conventional security measures will be key. By leveraging AI to analyze vast datasets for suspicious activities or anomalous behaviour, cybersecurity experts can significantly enhance their protective capabilities. This proactive approach not only addresses emerging threats but also ensures that cybersecurity strategies align with an increasingly AI-driven technological world.

1.3 Intersection of Cyber Security and AI

Artificial Intelligence (AI) is rapidly transforming the landscape of cyber security, fundamentally altering how professionals approach risk mitigation. Traditionally, cyber security relied heavily on predefined rules and static defenses. However, AI enables the development of dynamic solutions that adapt to emerging threats in real-time. By analyzing vast amounts of data at lightning speed, AI systems can detect unusual patterns and behaviours that may signify a breach. This proactive approach helps security teams respond to incidents before they escalate, shifting the focus from reactive measures to preventive strategies.

As organizations increasingly embrace AI within their cyber defenses, several opportunities and challenges arise. On one hand, AI can automate repetitive tasks, freeing up human experts to concentrate on more complex issues that require nuanced understanding and creativity. For instance, AI algorithms can manage routine monitoring and alert staff only when a significant event occurs, thus enhancing efficiency. On the other hand, the integration of AI introduces its own set of challenges. Cyber attackers are also leveraging AI to develop sophisticated attacks, creating a continuous arms race between offensive and defensive strategies. Furthermore, the reliance on AI raises questions about transparency and accountability. How do we ensure that AI systems make decisions that align with ethical standards? Addressing these concerns is vital as the security community navigates this complex intersection of technology.

Professionals in cyber security must adapt to this evolving landscape by continuously updating their skill sets and remaining informed about AI advancements. One practical step is to actively seek training opportunities that emphasize the synergy between AI and cyber security. Understanding AI's capabilities and limitations empowers security experts to implement more robust defenses, aligning their strategies with the latest technological trends to safeguard systems effectively.

2. AI Technologies in Cyber Security

2.1 Machine Learning and Threat Detection

Machine learning, often abbreviated as ML, has become a crucial component in the landscape of cybersecurity, particularly in the area of threat detection. As cyber threats are evolving rapidly, traditional methods of identifying and responding to these threats are proving increasingly inadequate. Machine learning methodologies, including supervised and unsupervised learning, help security professionals develop models that can recognize patterns in data and differentiate between benign behaviour and potential threats. This capability allows for a more proactive approach in identifying anomalies and potential breaches before they escalate into significant issues. For instance, algorithms can be trained on vast amounts of historical data, enabling them to understand what constitutes normal behaviour for a network. Through this understanding, they can flag suspicious activities that deviate from the norm, thus alerting cybersecurity teams to potential vulnerabilities and breaches.

Numerous case studies illustrate the effectiveness of machine learning in threat detection. One notable example is the use of ML algorithms by major tech companies to detect phishing attacks. By analyzing email metadata and the content of messages, machine learning models can evolve to identify the subtle indicators of phishing attempts that may go unnoticed by traditional security measures. Another case study involves financial institutions implementing machine learning techniques to combat fraud. These organizations employ algorithms that analyze transaction patterns to identify anomalies that suggest fraudulent activities. The results have been impressive, leading to significantly reduced fraud losses and enhanced security measures. Furthermore, companies in the healthcare sector are utilizing machine learning to safeguard sensitive patient data from cyber threats. By evaluating access patterns and user behaviour, healthcare organizations can take timely actions to prevent data breaches effectively.

As AI continues to proliferate in everyday life, cybersecurity professionals must adapt to these advancements. Integrating machine learning into threat detection processes not only improves the speed and accuracy of identifying threats but also enables teams to prioritize their responses effectively. By adopting a data-driven mindset, cybersecurity experts can leverage the insights gained from ML models to enhance their defensive strategies. Investing in knowledge about machine learning applications in cybersecurity can provide a competitive edge, making it essential for professionals to stay informed and prepared for the future landscape of threats.

2.2 Natural Language Processing for Security Analysis

NLP plays a crucial role in analyzing security-related texts and communications by transforming unstructured data into a format that machines can understand. With the exponential growth of digital communication, vast amounts of information flow through various channels, such as emails, social media, and forums. NLP algorithms can sift through this content, identifying potential threats by detecting specific keywords and phrases that indicate malicious intent. For instance, these algorithms can evaluate the sentiment and context of messages to distinguish between benign conversations and those that might suggest criminal activity. By parsing through this data, cybersecurity professionals can gain insights into emerging threats, improving their response times and strategies. This capability to process and analyze natural language can drastically enhance human analysis, amplifying the effectiveness of security operations and leading to better-informed decisions.

NLP is particularly effective in detecting phishing attempts and malicious content, which are common tactics used by cybercriminals. Phishing attacks often utilize deceptive emails that mimic legitimate communications to trick users into revealing sensitive information. NLP can automatically flag such attempts by analyzing the language used, searching for common phishing indicators, or analyzing the structure of the communication. For example, algorithms can identify unusual phrasing, pressure tactics, or misspellings that suggest a lack of authenticity. Moreover, machine learning algorithms can be trained to recognize patterns in phishing attempts, honing their ability to identify new and evolving strategies employed by attackers. As these technologies evolve, the combination of NLP and machine learning creates a more robust defense against various forms of social engineering attacks, enabling cybersecurity teams to proactively combat threats before they escalate.

Understanding how NLP fits into cybersecurity will become increasingly essential for professionals in the field. As AI technologies advance, integrating NLP into daily security practices will contribute to more effective threat intelligence and incident response. Cybersecurity teams should consider adopting these tools to automate mundane tasks, such as scanning communications for threats, allowing them to focus on critical analyses and strategic development. With the rapid pace of AI innovation, staying ahead by leveraging NLP in security analysis will not only enhance security measures but also foster a proactive stance against future cyber threats.

2.3 AI-Driven Anomaly Detection

Anomaly detection is the process of identifying patterns in data that do not conform to expected behaviour. In the realm of cybersecurity, this is crucial. It enables security professionals to spot unusual activity that could indicate security breaches, fraud, or other malicious actions. Identifying these anomalies helps organizations take proactive measures to protect their networks, systems, and sensitive data. The consequences of ignoring these irregular patterns can be devastating, leading to data breaches, financial losses, and damage to reputation. As cyber threats become increasingly sophisticated, the ability to detect these anomalies rapidly and effectively is more important than ever.

Advanced AI techniques are enhancing the capabilities of anomaly detection significantly. Machine learning algorithms, for instance, can be trained on vast amounts of historical data to understand what normal behaviour looks like within a system. Once established, these models can continuously learn and adapt in real-time, enabling them to identify even the subtlest deviations from the norm. Techniques such as deep learning can enhance this process further by allowing for the analysis of complex, multidimensional data. By employing neural networks, it becomes feasible to uncover deeper insights that traditional methods might miss. With AI's capabilities in natural language processing and behavioural analysis, cybersecurity professionals can extract meaningful patterns from text, logs, and user behavior, making it easier to spot anomalies that might otherwise go unnoticed.

As AI technologies evolve, their integration into existing cybersecurity frameworks is not just beneficial; it's essential. Security teams can leverage AI-driven anomaly detection tools to optimize their defenses, streamline incident response, and enhance overall threat management. It's important for cybersecurity professionals to stay informed about these AI advancements and how they can be implemented to mitigate risks effectively. Incorporating AI into your strategy not only improves detection rates but also allows teams to focus on higher-level cyber threats, ensuring that businesses remain one step ahead in this ever-changing landscape.

3. Benefits of AI in Cyber Security

3.1 Enhanced Threat Response Times

AI significantly improves the speed and efficiency of threat response in cybersecurity. It achieves this by rapidly analyzing vast amounts of data to identify unusual patterns that may indicate a cyber threat. Traditional security systems often struggle with the sheer volume of data generated by organizations, but AI can sift through this information almost instantaneously. By employing machine learning algorithms, AI adapts and learns from emerging threats, making it possible to respond effectively even against unfamiliar attacks. Automated threat detection systems can provide real-time alerts, initiating predefined protocols to contain potential breaches before they escalate. This shift from manual to automated responses allows cybersecurity professionals to focus their efforts on strategy and improvement rather than on time-consuming initial investigations.

Statistics highlight the remarkable impact of AI on response times within the cybersecurity landscape. Studies have shown that organizations deploying AI tools have witnessed an average reduction in response times by up to 70%. For instance, a report indicated that while traditional detection and response mechanisms could take hours to days to identify and neutralize threats, AI-driven solutions can reduce that time to mere minutes or even seconds. This acceleration not only minimizes the potential damage from attacks but also enhances overall organizational resilience. Furthermore, as AI systems become more sophisticated, they have the potential to decrease the risk of human error, which is often a critical factor in security breaches.

Incorporating AI tools into cybersecurity strategies isn't just a matter of keeping up with technology; it's essential for staying ahead of increasingly complex threats. Cybersecurity professionals should be proactive in exploring how these improvements can be seamlessly integrated into their existing security frameworks. By leveraging tools that harness the speed and precision of AI, organizations can not only enhance their response times but also fortify their defenses against evolving cyber risks. Engaging with AI solutions will ultimately empower cybersecurity teams to stay one step ahead in a landscape where every second counts.

3.2 Predictive Analysis for Future Threats

Artificial Intelligence (AI) has advanced significantly and is now capable of analyzing vast amounts of data to identify patterns and trends within the realm of cybersecurity. By leveraging machine learning algorithms, AI systems can monitor network traffic, user behaviour, and even the methods employed by cybercriminals over time. This capability allows organizations to stay one step ahead by predicting potential cyber threats before they materialize. AI can sift through historical data and real-time information to detect anomalies that may indicate an attack is in progress. Moreover, it can analyze how these anomalies correlate with past incidents, providing valuable insights that help security teams focus their efforts on the most likely threats. This proactive approach transforms cybersecurity from a reactive stance to a more anticipatory one, enabling businesses to reinforce their defenses before possible breaches occur.

Real-world examples illustrate how predictive analysis through AI has already made a significant impact on cybersecurity strategies. Companies such as Darktrace have developed systems that learn from network behaviour to identify emerging threats in real-time. For instance, during the COVID-19 pandemic, many organizations shifted to remote work, which introduced new vulnerabilities. AI-driven solutions were rapidly deployed to monitor for unusual patterns indicative of potential attacks targeting remote access points. Another notable case is the use of predictive analytics by the banking sector, where financial institutions implement AI to assess transaction patterns and flag potential fraudulent activity before it impacts customers. These instances reveal the tangible benefits that AI can bring to security operations, showcasing how predictive analysis is enhancing the ability to counteract threats effectively.

As AI continues to evolve and integrate into existing cybersecurity frameworks, professionals in the field should strive to understand these tools and adapt their strategies accordingly. Leveraging AI for predictive analysis not only fortifies defenses but also allows for the efficient allocation of resources. Organizations will benefit from adopting a mindset geared towards proactive threat management, making use of AI's analytical power to anticipate and neutralize cyber risks before they escalate. Whether it's through learning patterns in user behaviour or identifying shifts in the tactics of attackers, staying ahead of potential threats hinges on embracing these technologies.

3.3 Automation of Routine Security Tasks

Identifying repetitive security tasks that can be automated using artificial intelligence is crucial for improving efficiency in the cybersecurity landscape. Various tasks, such as monitoring system logs, conducting vulnerability assessments, and managing incident responses often demand significant time and attention from security professionals. Automation can streamline these processes by using machine learning algorithms and AI systems capable of analyzing vast amounts of data far beyond human capability. For example, AI can quickly sift through thousands of logs to identify unusual activity, flagging potential threats for further investigation. Additionally, automating software updates and patch management can ensure that systems stay secure without constant manual oversight. By identifying which repetitive tasks can be handled by AI, security teams can redirect their effort toward more complex challenges that require human intuition and expertise.

Examining the benefits of automation reveals how it can free security professionals for more strategic work. When routine tasks are automated, professionals can focus on proactive measures, such as threat hunting, developing security policies, and improving overall organizational security posture. Without the burden of tedious manual checks and updates, cybersecurity teams can dedicate their skills towards analyzing emerging threats and adapting frameworks to defend against new vulnerabilities. This shift not only enhances productivity but also improves job satisfaction, as professionals are likely to find greater fulfilment in tackling high-impact projects rather than getting lost in monotonous routines. Ultimately, integrating AI into routine security tasks promotes a more dynamic and responsive approach to cybersecurity, allowing teams to stay a step ahead of potential attackers.

One practical tip for security professionals is to start small by selecting a few repetitive tasks that can be automated using AI tools available in the market today. Start with tasks that consume a significant amount of time but pose a low risk, such as automating report generation or incident ticketing. Gradually expand automation efforts based on initial results, allowing the team to adapt to the changes while building trust in the technology. By measuring the impact of these automated processes, professionals can make more informed decisions about where to invest in AI tools, ultimately leading to a more resilient cybersecurity strategy.

4. Challenges of Implementing AI in Cyber Security

4.1 Data Privacy Concerns

The rise of artificial intelligence brings significant implications for data privacy and compliance with existing regulations. As AI systems increasingly analyze vast amounts of personal data to improve services, they inadvertently raise concerns about how this information is collected, stored, and utilized. Regulations such as the General Data Protection Regulation (GDPR) set strict guidelines on personal data usage, emphasizing the importance of transparency, consent, and security. Cybersecurity professionals need to navigate these regulations carefully while integrating AI solutions into their organizations. Failure to comply can result in heavy penalties and damage to reputation. Moreover, organizations must consider how AI algorithms could reinforce biases if the training data is not handled ethically. Therefore, as AI continues to evolve, maintaining compliance while fostering innovation will be a balancing act for cybersecurity experts.

To ensure data privacy while leveraging AI technologies, it is essential to adopt a multifaceted approach. One critical measure is implementing data minimization practices, where only the necessary data is collected and analyzed for AI processes. This reduces the risk of exposure and misuse of sensitive information. Additionally, incorporating advanced encryption techniques can safeguard data both in transit and at rest, creating layers of security that deter unauthorized access. Regular audits and assessments can help organizations identify potential vulnerabilities within AI systems, ensuring that any weaknesses are addressed promptly. Furthermore, promoting a culture of privacy within organizations can motivate employees to adhere to best practices concerning data handling and security. Training can greatly enhance awareness of data privacy issues, empowering staff to recognize and report potential breaches proactively.

Proactively addressing data privacy concerns in the realm of AI is not only a regulation compliance issue but also a competitive advantage in today's marketplace. Organizations that demonstrate a genuine commitment to protecting user data build trust with their clients, fostering customer loyalty in the long run. As a best practice, it's essential that cybersecurity professionals continuously engage in education and training regarding the latest privacy-focused technology and strategies. They should also stay abreast of evolving regulations to adapt their policies and practices accordingly. This proactive stance on data privacy not only mitigates risk but positions organizations as industry leaders committed to responsible AI deployment.

4.2 Bias in AI Algorithms

Bias in training data can significantly influence how AI systems make decisions, especially in the field of security. AI algorithms learn from historical data, and if that data contains biases—whether from human prejudice, under-representation of certain groups, or flawed data collection methods—those biases can manifest in the decisions made by AI. For example, if a security algorithm is trained predominantly on data that includes examples from only a specific demographic, it may inadvertently discriminate against others, leading to increased false positives or negatives for those groups. This can have serious implications in cybersecurity, where accurate threat detection is crucial for protecting sensitive information and maintaining trust.

Addressing and mitigating bias is essential for ensuring fair AI implementation in security contexts. One effective strategy is to ensure that training datasets are diverse and representative of all populations and scenarios that the AI may encounter. Regular auditing of AI systems can also help identify and correct biases by evaluating how algorithms perform across different demographics. Additionally, engaging a diverse team of experts during the development of AI solutions can provide varied perspectives, helping to recognize potential biases early in the process. Consistent monitoring post-deployment is critical as well, as real-world data may reveal biases not apparent during the training phase.

Practical tips for cybersecurity professionals include implementing bias detection tools and methodologies in their AI systems. Integrating fairness checks into the AI development lifecycle can help detect bias at early stages. Sharing knowledge about successful strategies for bias mitigation across professional networks can foster a broader understanding of this issue within the industry. By remaining proactive about recognizing and addressing bias, cybersecurity professionals can harness the power of AI while ensuring that their systems remain equitable and effective for all users.

4.3 Integration with Existing Security Frameworks

Integrating AI with traditional security systems involves navigating a complex landscape filled with both technological and procedural challenges. Traditional security frameworks have been built on rules-based approaches that rely heavily on defined parameters and known threats. However, AI introduces a level of adaptability and dynamism that can be at odds with these established systems. Implementing AI requires a thorough understanding of the legacy systems in place, their architectures, and how they process data. The challenge lies in ensuring compatibility and minimizing disruptions. Moreover, the sheer volume of data that AI systems can analyze must be harnessed in a way that augments traditional security protocols rather than overwhelms them. This often calls for a reassessment of current security processes, including how teams interpret alerts, respond to incidents, and manage logs. Integrating AI isn't merely adding a new tool; it's about rethinking how security is approached as a whole.

To facilitate a smooth integration of AI into existing security frameworks, several best practices should be considered. First, start with a clear strategy that aligns AI capabilities with the specific needs of your organization. It's essential to identify which areas of security would benefit most from AI, such as threat detection or automated response. After establishing these objectives, ensure that there is a shared understanding across teams. Collaboration between data scientists, cybersecurity professionals, and IT departments can drive better results and foster an environment of shared knowledge. The training phase is equally crucial; AI models must be carefully trained on relevant datasets to ensure their effectiveness while minimizing false positives. Furthermore, continuous monitoring and iterative updates are vital. AI systems should not be considered a one-and-done solution; they require ongoing evaluation and tuning to adapt to new threats and changing environments. This hands-on approach will not only enhance the effectiveness of the AI but will also build trust among the stakeholders who rely on these systems for their safety.

Embracing AI in cybersecurity is not just an upgrade but a transformation of mindset. Keeping pace with evolving threats in the cyber realm means blending traditional strategies with innovative technological advancements. Organizations should foster an adaptable culture that encourages experimentation and learning from both successes and failures. As cybersecurity professionals, understanding the nuances of AI and its implications on existing frameworks will position teams to better defend against emerging threats. Regular training sessions on new AI tools and technologies can ensure that personnel stay equipped and informed. By leveraging AI's capabilities while respecting the cornerstones of traditional cybersecurity practices, organizations can create a robust defense that is both proactive and resilient.

5. AI and Cyber Threat Landscape

5.1 Evolution of Cyber Attacks with AI

Artificial Intelligence is transforming not just how we live, but also how cyber attacks are executed. It allows cybercriminals to develop more sophisticated techniques, enabling them to exploit vulnerabilities in systems more efficiently. AI can analyze massive amounts of data far faster than a human, pinpointing weaknesses to exploit and automating tasks that used to require human intervention. For instance, AI-driven malware can adapt its behavior based on the security measures it encounters, making it significantly harder to detect. By mimicking human decision-making processes, it can trick security systems and go unnoticed until significant damage is done. This evolution signifies a paradigm shift in the cyber threat landscape, compelling professionals in cyber security to rethink and recalibrate their defensive strategies.

Several recent high-profile cyber attacks illustrate the potential for AI-enhanced tactics. One notable example is the 2020 Twitter hack, where attackers used social engineering techniques aided by AI to gain access to the accounts of high-profile individuals. They crafted convincing messages and may have even employed AI algorithms to analyze public interaction patterns, making their phishing attempts more effective. Similarly, the SolarWinds attack showcased how cybercriminals could infiltrate corporate networks by embedding malicious code into software updates—an operation made easier by AI's ability to camouflage harmful activities within legitimate processes. These attacks underline the urgent need for cyber security experts to leverage AI for defense as well, incorporating machine learning algorithms that can analyze patterns and detect anomalies more efficiently than traditional methods.

As the landscape of cyber security continues to evolve with AI, professionals must adopt a proactive stance. Investing in AI-driven security solutions can enhance threat detection and response times, allowing teams to mitigate risks before they escalate. Understanding the dual nature of AI—as both a tool for cybercriminals and a potential ally in defense—will become essential for those working in this field. Continuous learning and adaptation to new AI capabilities will be key. Staying informed about the latest developments in cyber threats and enhancing technical skills in AI applications will better equip cyber security professionals to protect their organizations against increasingly sophisticated attacks.

5.2 AI-Powered Malware and Ransomware

The emergence of AI-driven malware marks a significant evolution in the landscape of cyber threats. Cybercriminals now have access to sophisticated technologies that allow them to automate and optimize their attacks. These AI systems can learn from previous interactions, analyze data in real-time, and develop tactics that are tailored to individual targets. With the ability to predict and adapt to defenses, AI-enhanced malware can bypass traditional security measures much more efficiently than its non-AI counterparts. This evolution implies that organizations must rethink their security protocols, as the conventional reactive approach may no longer suffice. Companies need to implement proactive and adaptive strategies that leverage AI in their defense mechanisms, including continuous monitoring and learning algorithms to anticipate and neutralize potential threats.

Trends in ransomware attacks utilizing AI are pointing towards an alarming increase in their sophistication and impact. Ransomware operators are increasingly employing machine learning algorithms to identify vulnerabilities in their targets, deciding the best timing and method for execution. These attacks often leverage social engineering techniques powered by AI to create convincing phishing messages tailored to the specific interests of victims. The use of AI not only amplifies the effectiveness of these attacks but also boosts the attacker's ability to evade detection. Analyzing trends, it's clear that organizations must enhance their understanding of how AI influences these threats. This understanding enables them to formulate comprehensive security measures that address the ever-evolving tactics of cybercriminals.

As AI continues to integrate into everyday life, its implications on cybersecurity will undoubtedly grow. For professionals already in the cyber security field, staying ahead of this curve is crucial. Continuous education and hands-on experience with AI technologies can empower security teams to build resilient defenses. Collaborating with data scientists to develop AI-driven cybersecurity solutions can be beneficial. Remember, investing in AI-enhanced tools today could vastly improve your organization's ability to fend off future attacks and maintain cyber resilience.

5.3 Social Engineering and AI

AI is increasingly enhancing social engineering efforts by allowing attackers to manipulate human psychology at an unprecedented scale. The use of machine learning algorithms enables bad actors to analyze vast amounts of data from social media and other online platforms, creating detailed profiles of potential targets. This profiling enhances their ability to tailor messages or approaches that are more likely to succeed in deceiving individuals. For instance, sophisticated AI tools can generate convincing phishing emails or mimic the communication style of a legitimate company, making it difficult for targets to discern the authenticity of the message. The automation of these processes not only increases the efficiency of social engineering attacks but also reduces the time and resource investment necessary for attackers, leading to a higher frequency of incidents.

Several tactics are deployed in AI-enabled social engineering attacks that take advantage of human vulnerabilities. One prevalent tactic is the use of deepfake technology, where videos or audio recordings are manipulated to create realistic impersonations of trusted figures, often used to trick employees into transferring funds or divulging sensitive information. Additionally, AI can automate the generation of social media profiles that appear genuine, which can then be used to establish trust with targets. Moreover, natural language processing allows for the crafting of personalized messages that can resonate on an emotional level, increasing the likelihood of compliance from unsuspecting victims. Attackers can leverage AI to test different approaches rapidly, learning in real time what works and what doesn't, which makes each subsequent attack potentially more effective.

Understanding these evolving methods is crucial for cybersecurity professionals. One practical tip for organizations is to invest in AI-driven training for employees. By using simulated phishing attempts that utilize AI techniques, businesses can enhance their employees' ability to recognize suspicious activities, strengthening the human element of their cybersecurity defenses. Awareness and training can serve as a buffer against the sophisticated tactics that AI-powered social engineering brings to the forefront.

6. Ethical Considerations in AI for Cyber Security

6.1 Accountability of AI Systems

The integration of AI systems into everyday life has raised essential concerns regarding accountability, particularly in the realm of security. As these systems begin to influence critical decision-making processes, the assurance that they operate transparently and ethically becomes vital. In the context of cyber security, this need for accountability translates to ensuring that AI-driven actions are traceable and subject to scrutiny. A lack of accountability can lead to wide-ranging implications, such as data breaches or unauthorized access, where the source of the error is obscured by the complexity of the algorithms. Thus, establishing clear accountability in AI actions is not just a matter of compliance; it is a foundational requirement to maintain trust and security in systems that increasingly govern sensitive information.

Examining frameworks for assigning responsibility in AI-driven decisions reveals the complexity of accountability in this rapidly evolving field. Various models have been proposed, ranging from a shared responsibility approach to a more centralized accountability structure. When AI takes actions based on learned data, it's crucial to identify who is responsible when those actions lead to adverse outcomes— whether it be the developers, the organizations deploying the technology, or even the AI itself in some theoretical frameworks. These discussions emphasize the urgency for regulations that define liability and oversight mechanisms. Cyber security professionals must advocate for and engage with these frameworks, ensuring that they align with ethical standards while recognizing the unique challenges posed by AI.

As AI continues to transform the landscape of cyber security, professionals in this field should prioritize staying informed about these developments. Understanding the implications of AI on security protocols, data handling, and regulatory changes is essential. Regular training and involvement in discussions about AI accountability will prepare cyber security experts to effectively incorporate AI technology into their strategies while navigating the associated risks. Adopting a proactive approach in learning about AI implications can help security professionals provide better protection and develop more resilient systems.

6.2 Ethical AI Frameworks for Security

The deployment of artificial intelligence in security contexts raises significant ethical considerations that professionals in the field must navigate. Ethical guidelines are increasingly essential as AI technologies are integrated into security systems, impacted by their potential to influence decision-making processes. Issues such as bias in algorithms, data privacy, and the transparency of AI systems come to the forefront. Security practitioners must recognize the moral implications of AI, ensuring that the technologies employed do not perpetuate biases or lead to unjust outcomes. For instance, systems designed to detect threats should be scrutinized for fairness, examining how data is collected and how it might reflect existing inequalities. Establishing comprehensive ethical guidelines involves balancing technological advancements with a commitment to human rights, requiring professionals to engage with frameworks that advocate for responsible use of AI in security.

Several organizations are championing the cause of ethical AI practices, each contributing to the discourse around responsible AI deployment. The Partnership on AI, a collaborative initiative that brings together academia, industry leaders, and civil society, works to foster discussions on AI's benefits and challenges. Their focus on developing guidelines for ethical AI use is pivotal for cybersecurity professionals who must align their practices with evolving standards. Another notable entity is the IEEE Global Initiative on Ethics of Autonomous and Intelligent Systems, which aims to ensure that AI technologies are developed in a manner that respects privacy and promotes accountability. These organizations play an important role in shaping policies and best practices that security professionals can integrate into their operations, helping to create a robust framework for ethical AI deployment in the ever-evolving landscape of cybersecurity.

To remain ahead in the cyber domain, practitioners should actively engage with these ethical frameworks, taking the initiative to assess their AI tools against established guidelines. This proactive approach not only enhances their organization's cybersecurity posture but also fosters a culture of responsibility. Professionals should also consider ongoing education in ethical AI principles, utilizing resources from advocacy organizations to stay informed about new developments. As AI continues to evolve, understanding its ethical implications will be crucial for anyone in the field, ensuring that they not only defend against cyber threats but also uphold the integrity of the systems they protect.

6.3 Balancing Security and Privacy

The ongoing tension between enhancing security and maintaining user privacy stems from the increasing reliance on digital technologies, particularly in the realm of artificial intelligence (AI). As cyber threats continue to evolve, organizations are compelled to implement more robust security measures. However, these measures often require extensive data collection and monitoring, which can encroach on individual privacy rights. This creates a delicate balance where security efforts may inadvertently undermine users' trust and expose sensitive information. Consequently, cybersecurity professionals face the challenge of safeguarding systems while respecting the privacy of individuals. This dilemma becomes particularly pronounced as AI systems, designed for advanced threat detection and response, require vast amounts of data. The paradox lies in the fact that the very data used to enhance security can lead to reduced privacy for the end user, creating a cycle of distrust and concern about how their information is being utilized.

Achieving a balance between security and privacy involves implementing strategies that are both effective and respectful of user rights. One crucial approach is the adoption of privacy-by-design principles, where privacy considerations are integrated into the development of security systems from the outset. This means that organizations should assess the potential privacy implications of their security practices and strive to minimize data collection to only what is necessary. Transparency is another key factor; organizations that clearly communicate their data handling and security measures to users can foster trust and encourage cooperation. Furthermore, employing techniques such as data anonymization and encryption can help protect sensitive information while maintaining the utility of collected data for security purposes. Additionally, enhancing user control over their data through simple and accessible privacy settings empowers individuals and aligns with ethical security practices. Training cybersecurity professionals to be aware of and prioritize these considerations can transform the landscape, allowing AI to be leveraged effectively without compromising the fundamental right to privacy.

To navigate the complexities of balancing security and privacy, cybersecurity professionals should consider adopting tools that provide real-time insights without excessive data collection. For example, deploying machine learning algorithms that can detect anomalies based on patterns rather than monitoring every individual action can reduce the intrusiveness of security measures. Regular audits of both security protocols and privacy practices can also identify areas for improvement, ensuring that both domains evolve in tandem. Staying current with regulations and standards related to privacy can help organizations align their practices with legal requirements while also respecting individual rights. Ultimately, cultivating a culture of security awareness among all employees can ensure that everyone plays a role in maintaining this balance, fostering a more secure and privacy-conscious environment.

7. AI Tools for Cyber Security Professionals

7.1 Overview of Leading AI Security Tools

As artificial intelligence continues to integrate into various aspects of our lives, it has also become a vital part of the cyber security landscape. A number of prominent AI tools are reshaping how organizations defend against cyber threats. Tools such as Darktrace, CrowdStrike, IBM Watson for Cyber Security, and SentinelOne have emerged as key players. Darktrace utilizes machine learning to detect anomalies in network behaviour, allowing it to respond to threats in real-time. CrowdStrike's Falcon platform combines endpoint protection with threat intelligence, leveraging AI to predict and prevent attacks before they happen. IBM Watson enhances security operations by analyzing vast amounts of data to identify potential vulnerabilities and suggest remediation measures. Meanwhile, SentinelOne employs an autonomous response system that uses AI to remediate threats instantly, minimizing human intervention and thus reducing response times significantly. These tools represent just a snapshot of the rich ecosystem of AI-driven solutions that are transforming the cyber security landscape.

Each of these tools brings unique features and benefits to the table. Darktrace, for instance, is known for its ability to learn from the environment it protects, creating a self-learning approach that adapts to evolving threats without requiring manual updates. This allows organizations to stay ahead of potential attacks. CrowdStrike excels in providing detailed threat intelligence, ensuring that organizations not only respond to threats but also understand their origin and nature. Its cloud-native architecture allows seamless onboarding and integration, making it easy for teams to deploy. IBM Watson's greatest strength lies in its cognitive analysis capabilities, which can parse through billions of data points to surface actionable insights. This allows security teams to prioritize issues effectively, focusing on the most critical vulnerabilities. SentinelOne's ability to offer real-time incident response is revolutionary; by automating threat remediation, it reduces downtime and the potential for human error, enabling security teams to refocus their efforts on strategic initiatives.

As AI continues to advance, cyber security professionals need to embrace these tools to enhance their operational capabilities. Understanding these solutions and how they can integrate into existing processes will be key for those looking to upgrade their defensive strategies. Familiarizing oneself with the strengths of each tool can lead to more effective threat detection and response, while ensuring compliance with both regulatory standards and the ever-evolving landscape of cyber threats. Adopting an adaptive mindset towards using AI tools can significantly bolster an organization's overall security posture.

7.2 Customizing AI Solutions for Specific Needs

In the evolving landscape of cybersecurity, the importance of tailoring AI solutions to meet specific organizational needs cannot be overstated. Each organization faces unique challenges, and a one-size-fits-all approach often falls short. Customization allows businesses to leverage AI in a way that enhances their security posture, addresses their vulnerabilities, and aligns with their operational goals. By analyzing specific threats, workflow practices, and existing infrastructure, organizations can implement AI solutions that are not only effective but also seamlessly integrate into their existing systems. This targeted approach ensures that AI tools are relevant and provide the maximum benefit, enabling security teams to focus on high-priority tasks instead of sifting through misplaced alerts and ineffective data. As AI technology advances, its ability to learn and adapt to specific environments allows organizations to cultivate a proactive defense strategy, anticipating threats before they become critical issues.

Case studies of successful customization highlight the potential of AI in various cybersecurity contexts. For instance, a financial institution faced with the challenge of frequent phishing attempts turned to a customized AI model. This model was engineered to analyze the unique patterns of attacks specific to their customers, significantly increasing detection rates. By integrating machine learning with existing security systems, the organization reduced the time taken to flag suspicious emails from hours to minutes, allowing their security team to respond faster and more effectively. In another example, a healthcare provider encountered a rise in ransomware attacks targeted at their sensitive patient data. In response, they developed an AI-driven solution that incorporated both heuristic analysis and behavioural profiling tailored to their data access patterns. This customization empowered the organization to identify abnormal user behaviours indicative of a potential breach, leading to pre-emptive measures that effectively mitigated threats.

To harness the full potential of AI in cybersecurity, professionals need to focus on understanding their unique organizational landscapes. Continuous assessment of security needs and threat landscapes must inform the development of customized AI solutions. Engaging with stakeholders to gather insights about the specific challenges faced can lead to more effective implementation. It is equally important to stay informed about advances in AI and cybersecurity, as these fields are rapidly evolving. Organizations should consider investing in training for their cybersecurity teams to ensure they can effectively work with customized AI systems, thus enhancing the overall capability of their cybersecurity strategies. Prioritizing customization is not just a matter of preference; it is becoming a necessity in an era where threats are becoming increasingly sophisticated.

7.3 Open Source vs. Proprietary Tools

When considering the landscape of AI security tools, it's crucial to examine the advantages and disadvantages of open-source versus proprietary options. Open-source tools provide a level of transparency that proprietary tools often lack. With open-source software, cyber security professionals can inspect the code, which fosters trust and allows for collaboration among a community of developers. Additionally, these tools can be cost-effective, as they usually do not require hefty licensing fees. However, open-source tools can sometimes come with the challenge of limited support. If issues arise, the community may not always provide timely assistance, leading to potential delays in addressing vulnerabilities. Furthermore, the reliance on community-driven updates can result in inconsistencies in quality and functionality, which may be a significant concern for environments with strict compliance requirements.

On the other hand, proprietary tools usually come with dedicated support and maintenance, ensuring that users receive timely updates and technical assistance. These tools often offer a polished user experience, with extensive documentation and customer service channels available. However, proprietary AI security tools can be a significant financial investment, which is not always feasible for every organization. They may also impose restrictions on their use, limiting customization or integration with other systems. For professionals in cyber security, the choice between these tool types can depend on the specific needs of their organization, the available budget, and the desired level of control over the security tools being used.

Choosing the right tools requires careful consideration of several factors. Professionals should start by assessing their organizational needs, including the scale of operation and unique security challenges. For smaller businesses operating on a tighter budget, open-source solutions may provide adequate capabilities to initially combat potential threats. Meanwhile, larger organizations with complex infrastructures might benefit from the robustness and comprehensive support typically associated with proprietary tools. It's beneficial to weigh the investment of time and resources for learning open-source tools against the established effectiveness of proprietary options. As AI continues to evolve and integrate into everyday life, staying informed about the capabilities of each tool type will be essential. Keeping up with community forums and user reviews can provide valuable insights and aid professionals in making informed decisions that align with their specific security goals.

8. Case Studies of AI in Cyber Security

8.1 Successful Implementations

Numerous case studies demonstrate the effective deployment of AI in the realm of cybersecurity, showcasing its transformative power. One notable example is the implementation of AI-driven threat detection systems by a leading financial institution. By leveraging machine learning algorithms, the organization was able to analyze vast amounts of transaction data in real-time, identifying anomalies that may indicate fraudulent activity. This proactive approach led to a significant reduction in financial losses and a marked improvement in customer trust. Another exemplary case is the integration of AI tools at a major healthcare provider. Here, AI systems were utilized to monitor network traffic and detect potential breaches. The AI continuously learned from emerging threats, adjusting its defenses accordingly, which resulted in a robust security posture against ransomware and other sophisticated attacks. These real-world implementations not only highlight efficiency in threat identification but also demonstrate AI's capability to strengthen response strategies.

Several key factors contribute to the success of these AI implementations in cybersecurity. Firstly, the quality of data plays a crucial role. Organizations that invest in clean, diverse, and extensive datasets enable AI systems to perform at optimal levels. The more accurate the data, the better the AI can distinguish between benign and malicious activities. Additionally, the collaboration between cybersecurity professionals and AI experts is vital. Successful deployments often feature teams where cybersecurity analysts work alongside data scientists to create models tailored to specific threats. This synergy ensures that the AI tools are equipped with the latest threat intelligence and context. Furthermore, organizations that foster a culture of continuous learning and adaptation see greater success. Cyber threats evolve rapidly, and so must the solutions designed to combat them. By maintaining agility in their cybersecurity strategies, organizations can effectively utilize AI to stay one step ahead of potential attackers.

For those in the cybersecurity field, leveraging AI technologies presents both opportunities and challenges. Embracing AI tools not only improves efficiency but also broadens the capability to deal with emerging threats. It is essential for cybersecurity professionals to stay informed about the latest AI advancements and understand how these technologies can integrate with existing security frameworks. Continuous education, whether through formal training, workshops, or self-study, is a practical step to ensure relevance in a rapidly evolving security landscape. Building a network with peers who are also experimenting with AI can provide new insights and shared experiences that will enhance your understanding and application of these powerful tools in cybersecurity.

8.2 Lessons Learned from Failures

Examining case studies reveals several notable failures of AI implementations in cyber security. One prominent instance includes the deployment of an AI-driven security system that misidentified benign network activity as a potential threat. This false positive rate not only consumed valuable resources but also led to unnecessary panic among the IT staff, causing them to divert attention from genuine security concerns. Another example involves a financial institution that integrated an AI-based fraud detection system which, due to insufficient training on diverse data sets, failed to recognize sophisticated forms of fraud that weren't prevalent during its training phase. The result was a significant financial loss and a dent in customer trust. Instances like these highlight the critical importance of understanding the context and nuances of the environments in which AI technologies are deployed.

Common pitfalls in these failed implementations often stem from a lack of comprehensive data analysis and insufficient testing before deployment. Many projects neglect the necessity of diverse data sets, leading to systemic biases in the AI's decision-making process. Additionally, an overreliance on automated systems can desensitize security teams to emerging threats, as they may become complacent in trusting the technology without sufficient oversight. Moreover, many organizations fail to involve multidisciplinary teams in the development phases, leading to misaligned objectives and ineffective solutions. These lessons underscore the value of rigorous pre-implementation assessments and continuous learning cycles to navigate the complex landscape of cyber security effectively.

As AI technologies continue to evolve, it is essential for professionals in cyber security to adopt a mindset focused on adaptability and critical evaluation. Engaging in ongoing training and interdisciplinary collaboration not only enhances the effectiveness of AI tools but also empowers teams to spot and rectify potential pitfalls before they escalate. Establishing metrics for success and encouraging open discussions about failures can foster an environment where innovation thrives while ensuring that security remains paramount. By viewing failures as opportunities for growth, cyber security professionals can better prepare for the future where AI plays an integral role in protecting vital information.

8.3 Comparative Analysis of AI Adoption

The adoption of AI in the cybersecurity sector varies significantly across different industries, reflecting varying degrees of urgency and resource availability in addressing cybersecurity challenges. For example, the financial services sector has been at the forefront of AI deployment, leveraging machine learning algorithms for detecting fraud, predicting suspicious activities, and managing risks. The speed at which these institutions have integrated AI tools not only helps them protect sensitive data but also positions them ahead of potential threats. On the other hand, the healthcare sector is gradually embracing AI, focusing on areas like patient data security and ransomware protection, yet faces a slower adoption curve due to strict regulations and the need for comprehensive data privacy practices. Industries like retail and manufacturing are also making strides, albeit at a more cautious pace, primarily implementing AI solutions for customer data protection and operational security, respectively. In contrast, the public sector has encountered significant challenges in AI utilization for cybersecurity, dealing with legacy systems and limited budgets, leading to slower adoption rates despite a clear need for advanced threat detection and response capabilities.

Several factors play a crucial role in determining the successful adoption of AI within cybersecurity frameworks. First, organizational culture significantly influences readiness to embrace new technologies; companies that foster innovation and adaptability tend to integrate AI more effectively. Additionally, the availability of skilled professionals who understand both AI and cybersecurity is critical; a lack of expertise can hinder implementation and optimal use of AI tools. Budget constraints are another vital consideration; organizations must allocate sufficient funds not only for technology acquisition but also for ongoing training and maintenance. Regulatory compliance also plays a major role since understanding the legal implications of using AI technologies is necessary for sectors like healthcare and finance, where sensitive data handling is paramount. Finally, collaboration between technology providers and end-users can enhance the adoption process, as feedback and tailor-made solutions can lead to more effective AI integration.

For professionals already in the cybersecurity field, understanding these dynamics is essential. As AI continues to evolve, staying informed about the latest tools and strategies for its implementation will be key to enhancing security measures. Embracing continuous learning, attending workshops, and collaborating with AI experts can provide valuable insights into effectively utilizing AI in your cybersecurity practices. This proactive approach ensures not only personal career growth but also contributes to the overall strengthening of cybersecurity frameworks in your organization.

9. Future of Cyber Security with AI

9.1 Predictions and Trends

As artificial intelligence continues to evolve and integrate into everyday life, its influence on the cyber security landscape is becoming more pronounced. Emerging trends in AI technology are poised to reshape how security systems are developed, implemented, and managed. One key trend is the increasing use of machine learning algorithms to detect anomalies in network traffic. These algorithms can analyze vast amounts of data in real time, identifying patterns that may indicate a security breach far more quickly than traditional methods. This capability will enable security professionals to respond more effectively to potential threats, minimizing possible damage and downtime.

Another significant trend is the rise of AI-driven security tools designed to automate routine tasks, allowing cyber security professionals to focus on more complex issues. As AI systems become more capable of handling basic threat assessments, professionals will shift from reactive to proactive strategies, anticipating vulnerabilities before they can be exploited. Furthermore, AI tools that simulate cyber attacks can help organizations better prepare for real-world scenarios, enhancing their overall resilience. As these technologies mature, so too will the relationship between AI and human cyber defenders, leading to a more collaborative approach to security.

Looking to the future, the practices of cyber security professionals will undoubtedly evolve with the integration of AI. Professionals will need to adapt their skill sets to work alongside advanced AI systems, gaining expertise not only in traditional cyber security measures but also in understanding the intricacies of AI algorithms. Ethical considerations will also come to the forefront as AI use in defense and offense raises questions around privacy, accountability, and decision-making. Staying informed about the latest advancements and preparing to incorporate AI tools into their workflows will be essential for professionals looking to stay ahead in this rapidly changing field. Embracing continuous learning and exploring new technologies will empower them to leverage AI to enhance their cyber security strategies effectively.

9.2 The Role of Human Oversight

In AI-driven security operations, human oversight is not just important; it is critical. As organizations increasingly adopt artificial intelligence to enhance their cybersecurity measures, the potential for automation to outperform human decision-making can lead to an over-reliance on algorithms. This reliance may inadvertently overlook the nuanced understanding that a human security expert possesses, especially in complex scenarios where context matters immensely. Cyber threats evolve rapidly, and while AI can analyze patterns at lightning speed, it lacks the intuition and ethical judgment that humans bring to the table. The expertise of cybersecurity professionals remains indispensable in interpreting AI-generated data, identifying false positives, and making informed decisions that align with an organization's unique security needs. Maintaining a balance between automated processes and human intervention is essential in creating a resilient security posture that is robust enough to combat sophisticated cyber threats.

Effective collaboration between humans and AI can be achieved through several strategies. Clear communication channels are paramount, fostering an environment where cybersecurity professionals feel empowered to question AI outputs and provide insights based on their experience. Training is another key component; ensuring that team members understand how AI tools function, their limitations, and their strengths will enhance synergy. Regularly scheduled simulations and exercises involving both AI tools and human teams can help build a routine of collaborative problem-solving, making it easier for teams to respond to real threats. Furthermore, creating a feedback loop where AI systems learn from human interventions can lead to continual improvement, ultimately enhancing security measures and reinforcing the human-AI partnership. Implementing these strategies ensures that while AI may execute specific tasks and analyze threats, human oversight guarantees that decisions remain judicious and contextually relevant.

As the integration of AI in cybersecurity continues to expand, it's vital for professionals in the field to embrace this technology without discarding the fundamental value of human intuition and expertise. Regular training sessions and workshops focused on AI developments can keep cybersecurity staff well-informed, allowing them to harness the full potential of AI in their daily operations. Engaging in continuous learning about both emerging threats and AI capabilities will empower cybersecurity professionals to remain one step ahead in the ever-evolving landscape of cyber insecurity.

9.3 How AI May Transform Security Roles

As artificial intelligence becomes an integral part of daily life, the landscape of cyber security is undergoing significant changes. The integration of AI technologies will lead to substantial shifts in job roles and responsibilities within the field. Security professionals will increasingly find themselves collaborating with AI systems, which are capable of analyzing vast amounts of data and identifying unusual patterns that human analysts might miss. Consequently, roles will expand from traditional monitoring and response duties to strategic positions where human insight and AI capabilities converge. Security analysts may transition into roles such as AI trainers or overseers, where their expertise is essential in enhancing AI systems' understanding of threats. This collaboration will not only change the day-to-day activities of security professionals but will also demand a deeper comprehension of AI algorithms and machine learning models.

To thrive in this AI-enhanced security landscape, professionals will need to embrace opportunities for upskilling and reskilling. This means acquiring new competencies that go beyond conventional cybersecurity training. Courses in machine learning, data science, and AI ethics will become increasingly relevant. Engaging in hands-on training that emphasizes the practical application of AI in security will allow professionals to remain competitive and relevant. Organizations are likely to facilitate this transition by providing access to training programs and certifications, creating a culture of continuous learning. For those currently in the field, seeking mentorship from AI experts or collaborating with tech teams can further enhance their understanding of AI applications in security. Such proactive approaches will prepare individuals not just to adapt but also to become pioneering leaders in the evolving cyber security realm.

10. Regulatory and Compliance Implications

10.1 GDPR and AI Systems

The General Data Protection Regulation (GDPR) presents significant implications for artificial intelligence (AI) systems, especially within the realm of cyber security. AI systems are designed to process vast amounts of personal data to identify patterns, detect anomalies, and enhance security measures. However, this capability also raises concerns regarding data privacy and compliance. Organizations must ensure that their use of AI respects the principles of transparency, data minimization, and purpose limitation outlined in GDPR. For instance, AI-driven models that utilize personal data for security analyses must have lawful grounds for data processing, be able to demonstrate how data is used, and ensure that individuals' rights to access and control their data are upheld. There is an intricate balance between harnessing the power of AI in enhancing cyber security while ensuring that privacy regulations are strictly followed. Failure to comply can result in heavy fines and damage to reputation, primarily if AI systems lead to unintended data breaches or misuse of personal information.

Organizations looking to comply with GDPR while implementing AI systems in cyber security must adopt several strategic approaches. First, a thorough data audit is essential to understand what data is being collected, how it is processed, and who has access to it. This audit helps identify personal data and ensures that only necessary data is processed in line with the regulation. It is also crucial to implement privacy by design and by default principles in AI system development. This means embedding data protection measures into the design phase of AI technologies and ensuring that pre-selected settings for data processing always prioritize privacy. Furthermore, conducting Data Protection Impact Assessments (DPIAs) can identify potential areas of risk in AI applications early in their development, providing organizations with the opportunity to mitigate those risks effectively. Continuous training for staff on GDPR requirements and AI ethics is another key component to ensure compliance becomes part of the workplace culture.

For professionals in cyber security, understanding the interplay between AI and GDPR will become increasingly vital. Compliance isn't just about adhering to regulations; it's about fostering trust with clients and users whose data is being handled. As organizations leverage AI for proactive measures against cyber threats, they must prioritize robust data governance practices to mitigate risk. Staying updated with both the capabilities of AI and evolving regulations will be crucial. Engaging with legal experts to interpret GDPR as it relates to emerging AI technologies can provide additional clarity and support in navigating these challenges, ultimately enhancing both security measures and regulatory compliance.

10.2 Industry Standards and AI in Security

Industry standards play a crucial role in the development of AI security tools. As artificial intelligence continues to integrate itself into various aspects of our daily lives, cybersecurity professionals face the challenge of ensuring these AI systems operate within acceptable boundaries. Standards foster an environment of trust and reliability, helping to mitigate risks associated with using AI technologies. They provide a framework that guides the design and implementation of security measures, enabling professionals to understand the best practices and benchmarks necessary for effective AI deployment. By adhering to these standards, organizations enhance their ability to protect sensitive data and manage threats more effectively. It's not just about following rules; it's about cultivating a culture of accountability and ethical responsibility in using advanced technologies, ensuring safety on a broader scale.

Several leading standards guide the ethical use of AI in cybersecurity, providing frameworks that address the ethical dilemmas and security challenges posed by these technologies. For instance, the IEEE Global Initiative on Ethics of Autonomous and Intelligent Systems promotes standards that help ensure that AI respects human rights and values while being used for security purposes. Additionally, the AI Ethics Guidelines, developed by the European Commission, emphasize the importance of accountability, transparency, and fairness in AI systems. These guidelines also promote the need for continuous monitoring and evaluation of AI technologies to prevent bias and ensure that they contribute positively to security frameworks. Understanding these standards is essential for cybersecurity professionals, as they offer insights into best practices for managing AI's complexities while safeguarding organizations from potential vulnerabilities.

As AI becomes increasingly prevalent, cybersecurity professionals must stay abreast of these industry standards and ethical guidelines. Engaging with these frameworks not only ensures compliance but also positions security practitioners as leaders in the responsible integration of AI within their organizations. Keeping informed about the evolution of these standards will empower professionals to implement security measures that enhance effectiveness while mitigating risks associated with emerging technologies. As AI continues to shape the cybersecurity landscape, staying committed to ethical practices and industry standards will ultimately serve as a foundation for securing the digital world.

10.3 Compliance Challenges with AI

Organizations face numerous compliance challenges when integrating AI technologies into their operational framework. One significant issue is the ambiguity surrounding existing regulations. Many current laws do not explicitly address AI, leaving companies uncertain about their obligations. This uncertainty can lead to inconsistent practices, potentially exposing organizations to legal risks. Additionally, the lack of standardized guidelines across jurisdictions complicates adherence to compliance, as organizations engaged in global operations must navigate a patchwork of regulations. Data privacy emerges as another concern, especially with laws like GDPR which require strict handling and processing of personal data. When AI systems use large datasets, the risk of non-compliance rises dangerously if organizations fail to implement robust data governance strategies. Furthermore, the opacity of AI decision-making processes creates challenges for transparency and accountability, complicating compliance with fairness and anti-discrimination laws.

Navigating the regulatory landscape effectively requires several strategic approaches. First, organizations should remain informed about evolving regulations around AI and data use. This involves regular engagement with legal experts and industry bodies to understand changes and emerging best practices. Developing a clear AI governance framework is essential, helping to align AI initiatives with compliance requirements. Organizations can also implement regular audits to assess compliance in AI systems, ensuring that any deviations from regulatory standards are identified and addressed promptly. Incorporating ethical considerations into AI development will not only enhance compliance but also build trust among users and regulators alike. Organizations can capitalize on emerging industry standards and frameworks designed for AI to guide their practices further, ensuring they do not just comply with regulations but also lead in responsible AI use.

Staying proactive is crucial when dealing with compliance challenges in AI. Consider creating a task force dedicated to monitoring the landscape of AI regulations, technological advances, and best practices. This team can swiftly adapt your organization's policies in anticipation of regulatory changes, reducing the risk of non-compliance as AI continues to evolve in the cybersecurity realm.

11. Training and Skills Development for Cyber Security with AI

11.1 Identifying Essential Skills for Professionals

To navigate the evolving landscape of cyber security, especially with the rise of artificial intelligence (AI), professionals must sharpen certain critical skills. Understanding AI technologies is essential, as these systems increasingly underpin a wide range of operations within the cyber security realm. Cyber security professionals should be adept at recognizing how AI can be a double-edged sword; while it enhances security measures by automating responses to threats, it also introduces new vulnerabilities. Proficiency in machine learning algorithms enables these professionals to assess patterns in data that could indicate a breach, while knowledge of natural language processing aids in analyzing vast amounts of unstructured data for potential threats. Additionally, a solid grasp of ethical considerations surrounding AI in cyber security is imperative, as misuse or biases in AI systems could not only jeopardize security but also raise legal and moral concerns.

The need for continuous skills assessment cannot be overstated in this rapidly changing technological landscape. As AI continues to advance, cyber security professionals must commit to ongoing education and training to stay ahead. Regular self-assessments allow individuals to identify gaps in their knowledge and adapt to new tools and techniques that emerge. Participating in workshops, obtaining relevant certifications, and engaging with professional communities are effective ways to ensure skills remain sharp and relevant. Moreover, organizations need to foster a culture that encourages learning, providing resources and opportunities for employees to evolve alongside technological advancements. This proactive approach helps professionals not only adapt to changes in AI but also anticipate future trends that may redefine the cyber security landscape.

A practical tip for cyber security professionals is to leverage AI-driven tools and platforms that offer analytics and insights specifically catered to threat detection and response. By familiarizing oneself with these tools, professionals not only enhance their immediate capabilities but also position themselves as valuable assets within their organizations, capable of integrating AI into a comprehensive security strategy.

11.2 Training Programs Incorporating AI

Many effective training programs are now integrating AI into their curricula, and this innovation is reshaping the landscape of cybersecurity education. For example, programs that utilize AI-driven simulations allow cybersecurity professionals to engage in realistic, scenario-based training. These simulations can mimic real-world cyber attacks, enabling participants to develop their skills in a controlled environment. This hands-on approach is vital as it helps learners make quick decisions under pressure, reflecting the high-stakes nature of their work. Furthermore, personalized learning pathways powered by AI adapt to the unique strengths and weaknesses of each participant. By assessing individual progress in real time, these programs optimize content delivery, ensuring that professionals receive targeted training that genuinely enhances their capabilities.

Collaborations between tech companies and educational institutions are becoming increasingly common, leading to advanced training solutions that keep pace with the evolving landscape of cybersecurity threats. These partnerships allow educational programs to stay abreast of the latest technologies, ensuring that the curriculum is relevant and practical. For instance, partnerships have led to the development of online courses that utilize AI tools to detect vulnerabilities in systems, providing professionals with the experience they need to tackle modern threats. By bridging the gap between academia and industry, these forward-thinking solutions help create a workforce that is not only knowledgeable but also adept at leveraging AI functionalities in cybersecurity practices. This synergy ultimately fosters an environment of continuous learning, where professionals can adapt and grow in their careers as technology advances.

Understanding how AI fits into the cybersecurity realm is vital for those already in the field. Staying informed about these training programs and the collaboration between institutions encourages ongoing skill development and adaptability. Engaging with AI tools, whether through formal education or self-study, will be pivotal for cyber professionals looking to stay relevant. Individuals can consider subscribing to industry newsletters or joining professional organizations to learn about emerging training opportunities and resources that emphasize AI integration in cybersecurity.

11.3 Continuous Learning in an Evolving Landscape

The rapid advancement of artificial intelligence is reshaping various fields, and cyber security is no exception. As AI technologies advance, they create both opportunities and challenges for those working in cyber security. New threats emerge daily, and traditional methods of defense may quickly become obsolete. Ongoing education is no longer optional; it is a necessity to stay relevant in an industry where the landscape changes so rapidly. Continuous learning becomes paramount, not just to understand how to protect data against emerging AI-driven threats, but also to leverage AI tools to enhance security measures. Professionals in cyber security must be proactive about gaining new skills and insights that keep pace with these advancements.

Many resources are available to support continuous learning and professional development in this dynamic environment. Online platforms, such as Coursera, edX, and Udemy, offer courses specifically focused on AI in cyber security. Participating in webinars and attending industry conferences allows professionals to network with experts, gaining firsthand knowledge about the latest trends and technologies. Engaging with professional organizations, such as ISC² or ISACA, provides access to a wealth of resources, from certifications to research papers that help hone your skills. Additionally, following relevant blogs, podcasts, and forums dedicated to AI and cyber security ensures that you stay informed about current events, threats, and best practices. By actively pursuing these opportunities for knowledge expansion, cyber security professionals can not only keep up with the evolving landscape but also position themselves as leaders in their field.

Take a hands-on approach to your learning by participating in practical exercises and simulations that mimic real-world cyber threats. Engaging with platforms offering Capture The Flag (CTF) challenges can refine your skills while providing insights into how AI can improve your responses to cyber threats. Forming study groups with colleagues or joining local cyber security meetups can create a collaborative learning environment, fostering discussion about strategies and tools available. With the significant impact AI will have on cyber security, embracing a mindset of continuous learning is essential for those looking to thrive in this exciting, evolving field.

12. AI in Incident Response and Management

12.1 Role of AI in Incident Detection

Artificial Intelligence plays a crucial role in the timely detection of security incidents by leveraging its ability to analyze vast amounts of data at incredible speeds. Traditional security measures often struggle with the sheer volume of incoming information, which can result in slow response times and missed threats. AI technologies, particularly machine learning algorithms, excel in identifying patterns and anomalies within network traffic and user behaviour. This capacity for real-time analysis allows AI systems to recognize potential threats almost as soon as they occur, significantly reducing the window of vulnerability for organizations. By integrating AI, security teams can receive alerts on suspicious activities instantly, enabling them to act quickly and mitigate damage before incidents escalate.

An example of AI's effectiveness can be seen in the case of a financial institution that experienced repeated phishing attempts targeting its customers. By implementing an AI-driven detection system, the bank enhanced its security posture remarkably. The system utilized natural language processing to scan email communications and identify phishing characteristics. It learned from historical data to recognize evolving tactics used by attackers. Following the implementation, the bank reported a 90% reduction in successful phishing incidents, showcasing how quickly AI can adapt to new threats. Another case involved a major retail company that faced frequent breaches due to compromised point-of-sale systems. The company deployed an AI solution that monitored transaction patterns in real time, identifying abnormal activities indicative of a breach. This proactive approach resulted in the identification of several incidents before they could cause significant financial loss.

These case studies illustrate that AI not only enhances detection capabilities but also improves the overall security strategy by providing actionable insights and reducing the burden on security personnel. As AI continues to proliferate, its integration will shape the future of cybersecurity, allowing professionals to focus on strategic tasks rather than being overwhelmed by routine monitoring. Keeping abreast of AI advancements can turn a security team from a reactive unit into a proactive shield against threats. Seeking ongoing training in AI applications relevant to cybersecurity can be beneficial, positioning professionals to leverage these tools effectively within their organizations.

12.2 Automating Incident Management Processes

Artificial Intelligence is transforming how organizations handle incident management by streamlining and automating processes that were once manual and time-consuming. With AI algorithms capable of analyzing vast amounts of data in real time, organizations can detect anomalies and potential threats much faster than traditional methods. By automating initial responses to incidents, such as alerts and ticket generation, teams can focus on more complex challenges instead of getting bogged down in mundane tasks. AI can continuously learn from past incidents, improving its ability to prioritize alerts based on severity and historical context, which helps reduce false positives. This shift not only enhances speed and efficiency but also provides cyber security teams with the insights to improve overall response strategies.

During high-pressure incidents, the benefits of automation become even more apparent. Effective incident management requires swift action, and AI can play a pivotal role by providing real-time data analysis and automated responses. This is crucial in scenarios where human error can lead to severe consequences. By automating routine decision-making processes, AI ensures a consistent and rapid response, minimizing downtime and damage. For example, in the event of a data breach, AI solutions can automatically isolate affected systems, limit access, and even initiate recovery protocols before human responders can fully assess the situation. This proactive approach not only helps contain the incident but also reduces the psychological strain on security teams, allowing them to operate more effectively under pressure.

The incorporation of AI into incident management not only enhances efficiency and response times but also creates an environment where cyber security professionals can work more strategically. By freeing up valuable time previously spent on repetitive tasks, teams can dedicate more effort to developing strategies and improving security postures. Embracing AI for incident management requires a shift in mindset, acknowledging it as a tool to augment human capabilities rather than replace them. Understanding how these technologies work and how to leverage them will be crucial for any cyber security professional aiming to stay ahead in this rapidly evolving landscape. Investing time in learning how to interact with and manage AI-driven systems can provide a significant advantage in maintaining organizational resilience against threats.

12.3 AI-Enhanced Reporting and Forensics

Artificial intelligence significantly enhances reporting accuracy and forensic analysis during cyber incidents. By automating data collection and analysis, AI can quickly sift through vast amounts of information, identifying relevant patterns and anomalies that would be nearly impossible for human analysts to spot within a reasonable timeframe. For instance, AI algorithms can recognize signs of a security breach or data exfiltration in real-time, enabling organizations to respond promptly and effectively. This immediate analysis not only helps in containing the damage but also provides detailed insights into the nature of the incident, leading to more informed decisions on how to address vulnerabilities. Additionally, AI can improve reporting accuracy by minimizing human error, providing standardized inputs that enhance the reliability of incident reports and making them easier to understand for stakeholders who may not be technically inclined.

Various AI tools are now available that enhance the investigative process in cyber security. Solutions like IBM's QRadar utilize machine learning to automate threat detection and response, improving both the speed and accuracy of investigations. Another notable tool is Palantir, which excels at data integration and visualization, allowing investigators to see connections and patterns they might not discern through traditional methods. Furthermore, platforms such as Nuix use AI to analyze unstructured data at great speed, helping forensic experts uncover critical evidence during investigations. These tools not only augment human capabilities but also enhance collaboration among cybersecurity teams by providing a centralized view of threat landscapes and incident timelines. As these technologies continue to evolve, cyber security professionals will need to adapt their skills and workflows, embracing AI as an integral part of their investigative toolbox.

Embracing AI tools can greatly expedite your incident response process. By integrating AI capabilities into your cyber security strategy, you can enhance your team's efficiency and improve overall security posture. Always stay updated on the latest AI developments; even simple automation can free your team to focus on more complex tasks.

13. Collaboration between AI and Cyber Security Teams

13.1 Integrating AI into Security Operations

Integrating AI into existing security operations demands careful planning and execution. A primary best practice is to assess the existing infrastructure and identify areas where AI can enhance efficiency and effectiveness. This involves understanding the specific security challenges faced by the organization and determining how AI technologies, such as machine learning and behaviour analytics, can address these issues. Implementing AI tools as augmentations to current processes rather than as a complete replacement will ensure a smoother transition and preserve the expertise of human operators. Additionally, training staff to work alongside AI, fostering an environment that encourages adaptation and innovation, is essential. Regular assessments and updates of the AI systems should also be scheduled, ensuring the technology evolves in tandem with emerging threats.

The collaboration between AI tools and human experts is where the true potential of cybersecurity lies. AI excels at processing vast amounts of data quickly, identifying patterns that may elude human analysts. However, the nuanced understanding of context that human professionals possess is irreplaceable. AI can automate routine tasks, freeing up human experts to focus on complex threats requiring critical thinking and creativity. This symbiotic relationship not only enhances operational efficiency but also enables security teams to tackle threats more proactively and effectively. Encouraging open communication between AI-generated insights and human decision-making fosters a culture that values both technology and human intelligence, leading to more informed security strategies.

Understanding that the successful integration of AI into security operations is an ongoing process is crucial. Regular training sessions that keep staff updated on both AI advancements and evolving cyber threats can create a culture of resilience. Staying informed about the latest research in AI and cybersecurity will empower professionals to harness AI's full capacity while contributing their unique expertise to the process. This dual approach can significantly strengthen an organization's overall security posture.

13.2 Team Dynamics with AI-Driven Tools

The introduction of AI tools is transforming team dynamics within cybersecurity in fundamental ways. Traditionally, cybersecurity professionals relied heavily on their individual expertise and collaborative discussions to tackle security threats. However, AI brings a suite of advanced capabilities that can analyze massive amounts of data far faster than any human could. As AI tools automate routine tasks such as log analysis or threat detection, team members are freed to engage in more strategic thinking and collaboration. This shift can lead to an enhanced focus on complex problem-solving rather than just keeping up with the demands of day-to-day operations. As a result, the roles within teams may evolve, requiring members to adapt to AI systems, learn to interpret AI-generated insights, and understand how these insights inform overall security strategy. The relationship between team members may also shift; individuals who once felt isolated in their roles can now leverage each other's AI-driven discoveries, fostering a deeper sense of collaboration and interdependence. Open communication about AI tools will become key, ensuring that every team member feels informed and empowered to contribute to decision-making processes based on AI insights.

Fostering teamwork and cooperation in this AI-enhanced environment requires intentional techniques. One effective approach involves integrating training programs that help team members understand the AI tools at their disposal and how to best utilize them. By proving ongoing education, teams can prevent feelings of inadequacy or fear around AI, ultimately cultivating a culture of confidence and innovation. Additionally, regular meetings that prioritize sharing experiences and discussing successes and challenges with AI can create a sense of transparency and collective achievement. Encouraging team members to collaborate on projects that leverage AI insights allows everyone to see the benefits firsthand, reinforcing the value of teamwork in achieving security objectives. Creating a feedback loop where team members can share how they use AI tools in their daily tasks can promote a culture of continuous improvement, where everyone learns from each other's experiences. Celebrating milestones and successes that result from collaborative efforts with AI tools can enhance team morale and recognition of each individual's contributions.

As cybersecurity continues to evolve in the age of AI, staying adaptable and open-minded is crucial for any professional in the field. One practical tip is to regularly set aside time for informal brainstorming sessions where team members can discuss new ideas on incorporating AI into their workflows. This open dialogue can lead to innovative applications of AI tools that enhance efficiency and effectiveness, ultimately strengthening the team's overall performance against cybersecurity threats.

13.3 Ensuring Communication and Feedback Loops

Communication is the backbone of any effective team, and this becomes even more critical when integrating AI into security operations. AI tools can analyze massive amounts of data and provide insights at speeds unattainable by human analysts alone. However, if the insights generated by these tools are not communicated effectively to the human members of the security team, the potential benefits can be quickly lost. Security professionals must cultivate an environment where information flows seamlessly, enabling team members to understand AI findings, ask questions, and discuss implications. Regular updates and clear reporting mechanisms should be established to ensure everyone is on the same page, fostering collaboration between human intuition and AI's prowess.

To maintain effective feedback loops in operational processes, establishing structured yet flexible communication pathways is key. Teams should consider using collaborative platforms that allow for real-time discussions and sharing of insights. Regular check-ins and debriefs can facilitate this exchange, allowing teams to review both the AI's recommendations and their own experiences during incident responses. Creating a culture where feedback is not only welcomed but actively sought out, encourages continuous learning and adaptation. For instance, after an incident, conducting a post-mortem analysis that includes input from both AI systems and human analysts can provide invaluable insights, helping teams refine processes and improve response strategies over time.

Incorporating AI into cybersecurity efforts brings new challenges and opportunities. It's worth noting that as part of this evolution, the role of human oversight is more crucial than ever. Teams should adopt practices like documenting the rationale behind decisions made, both from human and AI perspectives. This helps tie back AI decisions to human expertise and fosters trust in using these systems. Moreover, creating a practice of sharing success stories and learnings with the entire security team enhances morale and reinforces the collective effort. By ensuring a robust communication and feedback process, teams can not only harness the full potential of AI but also create a more resilient cybersecurity posture.

14. Measuring the Effectiveness of AI in Cyber Security

14.1 Key Performance Indicators for AI Security Tools

The essential Key Performance Indicators (KPIs) for evaluating the performance of AI security solutions play a crucial role in understanding how effectively these tools protect sensitive data and systems. One key indicator is the detection rate, which measures the percentage of threats successfully identified by the AI system compared to the total number of known threats. This metric helps organizations assess whether their AI security tools are capable of keeping up with evolving cyber threats. Another vital KPI is the false positive rate, which indicates how often legitimate activities are mistakenly flagged as malicious by the AI. High false positive rates can lead to alarm fatigue among security teams, making it crucial for AI solutions to strike a balance between sensitivity and accuracy. Response time is another KPI, tracking how quickly an AI system can react to identified threats. A rapid response time minimizes potential damage and enhances overall security posture. Furthermore, monitoring user behavior analytics reveals how well the AI adapts to normal user patterns and identifies deviations that could indicate a breach. All these metrics provide valuable insights that help inform decisions about ongoing investments in AI security technologies.

Aligning KPIs with organizational security objectives is essential for ensuring that AI security tools support broader business goals. Organizations should begin by clearly defining their security objectives, such as reducing response times to incidents, minimizing data breaches, or improving user awareness regarding phishing attacks. Each of these goals can then be directly linked to specific KPIs. For example, if an organization aims to reduce data breaches, they might focus on enhancing the detection rate of their AI solution, ensuring it is tuned to swiftly recognize even subtle anomalies. Regular communication between stakeholders, including security teams, IT staff, and upper management, is vital to ensure everyone is on the same page regarding objectives and expectations. It's also important to review these KPIs periodically as both organizational goals and the threat landscape constantly evolve. This adaptability will not only ensure that AI tools remain relevant but will also maximize their effectiveness in achieving the desired outcomes.

As AI becomes increasingly integrated into cybersecurity strategies, professionals need to stay informed about how these technologies can augment traditional approaches. Adopting a metrics-driven mindset and consistently analyzing key performance indicators allows organizations to fine-tune their AI tools continuously. Establishing a feedback loop where insights from KPI analysis feed back into the development and enhancement of AI security solutions can pave the way for more robust defenses against cyber threats.

14.2 Benchmarking Success

Examining methodologies for benchmarking the success of AI implementations in cyber security reveals the critical factors necessary for evaluating effectiveness. One approach involves defining clear key performance indicators (KPIs) that relate directly to specific AI capabilities. Measures such as threat detection rates, response times to incidents, and reduction in false positives can serve as vital metrics. Another useful method is to utilize a maturity model that assesses the progression of AI integration into existing security frameworks. These maturity models can gauge the organizational adaptation to AI, the complexity of deployed systems, and the overall improvement in security posture as a result of AI tools. Additionally, continuous monitoring and feedback loops should be established to analyze real-time data, allowing organizations to quickly adjust their strategies in response to evolving threats. In implementing these methodologies, it's also essential to include a comparative analysis against industry standards to understand where a company stands relative to its peers.

Several notable examples illustrate successful benchmark case studies of AI in cyber security. One case is that of a large financial institution that employed AI-driven anomaly detection systems. By integrating machine learning algorithms, the firm improved its threat detection rate by over 90%, significantly reducing the average time to identify and respond to incidents. Their benchmarking process entailed rigorous A/B testing against traditional detection methods, which not only validated AI effectiveness but also demonstrated cost savings associated with fewer breaches. Another case worth mentioning involves a leading telecommunications company that utilized AI to automate its incident response protocol. Through benchmarking against previous manual processes, they not only reduced response times by 60% but also substantially decreased the workload on their security analysts, allowing them to focus on more complex threats. These examples highlight that through the diligent application of benchmarking methodologies, organizations can effectively measure and enhance their AI capabilities in cyber security.

Leveraging AI is not just about technology; it also involves strategic thinking about how to best use these tools. For professionals in cyber security, it is crucial to continuously seek out new metrics that reflect the changing landscape of threats and technologies. Keeping abreast of industry advancements and emerging case studies can provide insights into how to implement and benchmark your own AI initiatives. Remember, the goal of benchmarking is not only about recognizing existing achievements but also about identifying areas for growth and improvement.

14.3 Continuous Improvement and Feedback Mechanisms

The landscape of AI security tools is marked by rapid advancements and evolving threats, making continuous improvement strategies essential. By fostering a culture of ongoing enhancement, organizations can ensure their AI-driven security solutions remain effective against adversaries who are equally adapting their tactics. Continuous improvement strategies involve regularly evaluating the performance of AI systems and incorporating lessons learned from past incidents. This approach not only helps in fine-tuning the algorithms but also enhances overall threat detection capabilities. By implementing regular updates, fine-tuning parameters, and leveraging new data sources, organizations can keep their AI systems relevant and robust. As AI solutions become an integral part of cybersecurity, a proactive mindset toward improvement will be critical in outpacing cyber threats.

Feedback mechanisms play a pivotal role in enhancing AI capabilities, solidifying the bond between human expertise and machine learning. Incorporating feedback from cybersecurity professionals is crucial, as they provide insights that can directly influence the development and refinement of AI tools. Regular collaboration between AI developers and cybersecurity teams creates a feedback loop where real-world experiences drive system enhancements. This interaction allows AI systems to learn from both successes and failures, leading to more accurate threat assessments and quicker response times. Moreover, incidents should be analyzed to determine what worked, what didn't, and why. This reflection process not only aids in improving existing AI algorithms but also inspires innovative features and functions that can better address emerging threats.

Understanding how to integrate continuous improvement and feedback mechanisms can greatly enhance the effectiveness of AI in cybersecurity. One practical tip is to establish a routine where AI performance metrics are reviewed against emerging threats every quarter. Such regular assessments enable security teams to adapt their strategies in line with both AI advancements and the shifting cyber landscape, ensuring that you remain several steps ahead of potential threats.

15. Conclusion: The Road Ahead for AI in Cyber Security

15.1 Summary of Key Insights

The integration of artificial intelligence into cybersecurity is leading to groundbreaking discoveries that fundamentally change how threats are identified and addressed. AI has proven to be invaluable in analyzing massive amounts of data at unprecedented speeds, enabling security systems to detect anomalies that would otherwise go unnoticed. Machine learning models can adapt and evolve based on the types of attacks they encounter, making them better equipped to respond to new threats as they arise. Furthermore, AI's predictive capabilities can help organizations foresee potential vulnerabilities and attack vectors, empowering proactive security measures rather than just reactive ones. This shift not only enhances the efficiency of identifying threats but also optimizes resource allocation, allowing cybersecurity professionals to focus on more critical tasks while AI handles routine monitoring and alerts.

As AI continues to reshape the landscape of cybersecurity, professionals in the field must adapt their skills and strategies to leverage these advancements effectively. Understanding AI's role in threat detection and response is essential for staying ahead in a rapidly evolving cyber threat environment. Continuous education on AI technologies and their applications in cybersecurity is crucial. Moreover, fostering collaboration between AI systems and human analysts is key, as the synergy between machine learning's data processing capabilities and human intuition can lead to better decision-making. Cybersecurity professionals should also prioritize developing a mindset oriented towards innovation and adaptability, as the constant evolution of AI will necessitate an ongoing commitment to learning and development in their careers. Keeping abreast of advancements in AI will not only enhance individual skill sets but also provide a competitive advantage in the field.

To navigate the integration of AI in cybersecurity successfully, it's beneficial for professionals to engage in cross-disciplinary training that combines traditional security knowledge with AI literacy. This might include workshops, online courses, or collaborative projects focused on real-world applications of AI in cybersecurity. By understanding the strengths and limitations of AI, professionals can effectively implement tools that augment their capabilities while ensuring that human judgment remains central to the decision-making process. This blend of technology and expertise will serve as a powerful strategy in combating the sophisticated cyber threats of tomorrow.

15.2 Future Challenges and Opportunities

The integration of artificial intelligence (AI) into cyber security presents significant challenges that professionals in the field must navigate. One of the primary concerns is the potential for adversaries to leverage AI themselves. Hackers can use AI tools to automate attacks, enabling them to probe systems more efficiently and discover vulnerabilities faster than traditional methods. As AI becomes more accessible, the possibility of AI-driven threats increases, making it crucial for security teams to stay ahead. Additionally, the complexity of AI systems can lead to unforeseen vulnerabilities that are difficult to detect and mitigate. Dependence on machine learning algorithms also raises questions about data quality and bias, which could inadvertently affect security measures. In a landscape where threats evolve rapidly, maintaining a secure environment becomes increasingly challenging, demanding continuous adaptation and skill enhancement from cyber security professionals.

Despite these challenges, AI offers remarkable opportunities to enhance security practices. With AI's ability to analyze vast amounts of data quickly, organizations can achieve more robust threat detection and response capabilities. AI algorithms can identify patterns and anomalies in network traffic, enabling quicker identification of potential security breaches. Moreover, automating routine tasks with AI frees up cyber security professionals to focus on more strategic initiatives, thereby improving overall effectiveness.

AI-driven predictive analytics can help organizations assess their vulnerabilities and anticipate potential attacks, allowing proactive defenses to be put in place. Implementing AI in security operations can lead to significant improvements in incident response times and a better understanding of evolving threats. As the work landscape shifts with the increasing integration of AI, professionals in cyber security must embrace and master these technologies.

To successfully incorporate AI into their security strategies, practitioners must prioritize continuous learning and skill development. Staying informed about the latest AI technologies, threat intelligence trends, and the ethical implications of AI is vital. Collaborating with data scientists and AI specialists can bridge the gap between traditional cyber security approaches and innovative AI solutions, fostering a holistic security strategy. Networking with peers in the AI domain can provide insights into effective AI applications for security, further enhancing the potential for proactive threat management.

15.3 Final Thoughts on Cyber Security and AI

The integration of artificial intelligence into the realm of cyber security represents a powerful synergy that is transforming how we protect sensitive data and infrastructures. AI enhances the detection and response capabilities of security systems, enabling quicker identification of potential threats. Machine learning algorithms can analyze vast amounts of data in real-time, identifying patterns that may indicate a cyber attack. As systems grow more complex, the ability for AI to process and analyze these complexities will become even more crucial. AI can also help mitigate human errors, which are often the weakest link in cyber security. By automating routine tasks and providing predictive analytics, AI allows security professionals to focus on strategic decision-making rather than getting bogged down in repetitive operational duties. However, as beneficial as these advancements are, they also come with challenges. Threat actors may leverage AI to develop more sophisticated attacks, requiring defenders to stay ahead of the curve by continuously evolving their strategies and tools.

In the face of an ever-evolving cyber landscape, it is essential for professionals in the field to embrace a mindset of continuous adaptation and vigilance. Cyber security is not a static field; it requires an ongoing commitment to learning as technologies and threats change. Keeping abreast of advancements in AI and understanding their implications for security practices will be key to remaining effective. Regular training and upskilling can empower cyber security teams to leverage AI tools successfully and to implement best practices that enhance their overall security posture. Engaging in collaborative information sharing with peers and industry leaders can further provide insights into emerging threats and countermeasures. This proactive approach will help organizations not only defend against current threats but also anticipate future challenges in a landscape where AI's role continues to grow.

Awareness of the benefits and potential dangers of AI in cyber security will be essential for practitioners. Those in the field should consider developing specialized skills in AI and machine learning to better navigate this intersection and enhance their careers. As the role of AI expands, embracing lifelong learning and adapting to new technologies will not only protect organizations from threats but also advance one's professional journey in the cyber security domain.